Modern Retirement Strategies

Modern Retirement Strategies

A Definitive Guide for Retiring Well

A Compilation of
Financial Industry Thought Leaders

Mark Edward Gaffney, Editor

LEON SMITH
PUBLISHING

ISBN: 978-1-945446-97-9

*To the hardworking American men and women
who sit at the table of sacrifice to save money for
that proverbial rainy day called* retirement.

Contents

Acknowledgments

First, I acknowledge the Lord for giving me the insight to put this book together.

I acknowledge the folks at the MEG team, without whose help this book would not be possible.

I acknowledge my family, my wonderful wife Jennifer Gaffney.

Lastly, I acknowledge all the authors in the book, whose tireless efforts help so many thousands of retirees and pre-retirees.

Introduction

Years ago, I started working with great financial advisors across the country—each telling their story of how they helped, respectively, tens of thousands of families to retire well, through good times and bad. It gave me the idea to collect from these advisors their number-one way to help folks retire well.

It became a passion—a vision, a movement—for me to interview advisors about their best stuff. I asked them to share what was most helpful for wherever retirees and pre-retirees are in their journey. This includes actions that could be relatively easy to take, but most importantly, to take what, for most people, are difficult concepts and put them in lay terms so the concepts could be understood. People could genuinely use the information to better their financial life and their families' financial lives.

In order to derive best results from this book, have pad and pen or highlighter with you because you will be given much information. Some of it is easy to assimilate; other pieces of information may take time.

I suggest a few strategies you can use to maximize the benefit of this book:

- Create a top ten list of gold nuggets from this book.

- Use those nuggets yourself if you handle your own retirement.

- If you work with an advisor, bring them to your advisor *right now*.

- Engage with the advisor who gave you this book so you can get all your questions answered.

Sometimes, even the smallest element you change in your retirement helps you move from a mediocre retirement to a great one. One small change can take you from a potentially failed retirement to having the retirement of your dreams. I challenge all of you to take the appropriate notes to get to where you want to go.

I hope this book will bring you peace of mind. Too many pre-retirees and retirees today worry about their money. Like them, you may find yourself asking questions like:

- *Will I have enough money to make it through retirement?*

- *Will I be able to handle all the unknown things that pop up from health care to grandkids' college educations to the air conditioning needing repair?*

- *Will I be able to travel and see my grandchildren?*

- *Will I be able to participate in my family's life?*

- *Will I be able to participate with my spouse in all the things on our bucket list?*

Use the wisdom in this book to create peace of mind in the golden years of your life.

~ Mark Edward Gaffney

401(k) and Other Pretax Savings: How Your Investment Decisions Today Can Affect Your Retirement Decisions Tomorrow

by Don Albach

The Two 'E's: Economics and Emotion

As an advisor, I'm surprised by how emotional clients can get regarding their 401(k). I recently met a couple who were so proud that they were to able save almost $2 million for retirement. Together they spoke about all the sacrifices they had made and things they had done without. Things like not purchasing new cars or taking extravagant vacations. They began to tell me how much money they had saved in income taxes over the years by deferring into his 401(k). I could tell by the gleam in their eyes how proud they were that they had taken advantage of these pretax contributions and built a nest egg for their retirement.

But now it was time to have *the tax conversation* and look at their IRAs and how they would fund their retirement. During the next few weeks, we explored where their income would come from. Upon review of the recommendations, they realized they would not need to take money from their IRAs, choosing instead to defer distributions as long as they could.

At age seventy-two-and-a-half, they would begin collecting their required minimum distributions. Based upon calculations using current rules, we were talking about another $60,000–$70,000 a year of income that, again, they didn't need to continue to live as they had before retirement. Based on current income tax rates, they also realized that their income tax bill would increase by an additional $20,000–$30,000 per year. I could see them doing the calculations in their heads, and they finally blurted out that they could potentially pay hundreds and thousands of dollars in income taxes over their retirement on the money they had saved.

Everybody's an Expert

Many of the people we meet with to do retirement planning are confused about what financial strategies they should be using. With so much information and misinformation available, people can feel overwhelmed when planning their retirement. They have heard on the radio that they should be following some specific financial strategy, such as maxing out their 401(k), or using a fifteen-year mortgage to pay their house off as soon as possible. Financial magazines often feature very broad, and sometimes conflicting, advice.

Recently, a popular financial magazine published an article on the twenty-five best locations to retire. However, on closer examination, we found that one of the recommended towns had a higher-than-the-national-average cost of living and had a higher state income tax rate than the national average. Therefore, it's so important that you work with an experienced licensed financial professional. In addition, you want to make sure you are working with a financial professional who is also a *fiduciary*—an ethical, trustworthy agent who acts on your behalf to manage finances.

People Follow Easy Advice

When it comes to retirement planning, or financial planning in general, many people feel overwhelmed by what they should be doing or where they should begin. Many times, we meet clients whose financial plan was simply to max out their pretax 401(k) or other pretax retirement plan and pay their house off early.

Both financial strategies are easy; 401(k) contributions come out of your paycheck pretax, systematically and are automatically invested. A fifteen-year mortgage can be put on automatic monthly withdrawal, and you're on your way to paying off your house.

While paying off a home early may seem like a great financial strategy, real-estate values may decline. In addition, if you need access to the equity in your home, you will have to borrow against the equity from a bank or lending institution.

That is why you should have a financial plan. A financial advisor can help you with your planning and can show you the best path, even if it is not the easiest path.

Consequences: What Looks Good Today Might Not Be Good Tomorrow

As part of our retirement planning process, we work with our clients on their estate and legacy planning. As discussed earlier in this chapter, we often meet clients who will not spend all their traditional IRA money in retirement. And when we educate them on how traditional IRA assets are taxed when children and grandchildren receive the money, many of them are dumbfounded. When a traditional IRA is inherited by the children or other heirs, the party inheriting is responsible for the income taxes due.

In 2019, Congress passed the "Secure Act" that has changed the tax law on how IRA accounts are taxed and have eliminated the Stretch IRA benefit. While your children can defer paying the tax on the inherited IRA for up to ten years, ultimately, they will have to pay the income taxes on the inherited IRAs.

More importantly, with our national debt skyrocketing and politicians talking about 60, 70, or 80 percent income tax brackets in the future, it is extremely important that you develop an exit strategy out of your pretax IRA or 401(k) accounts. If you are concerned about leaving a legacy and have accumulated a substantial account balance in your pretax retirement accounts, you must be aware that taxation on these accounts could be devastating to your heirs.

Doing Things Wisely in Today's Economy

We strongly advise you to educate yourself about retirement planning, especially in today's environment, with the complicated tax code and the changing economic state and the global economy we live in.

Be sure to explore issues such as:

- How do Roth IRAs compare with traditional IRAs?

- Do I pay a little bit more tax today to have a tax-free retirement in the future?

- Where do I save—do I save in investment accounts that I set up myself, or do I work with an advisor?

It may not be enough to invest only your 401(k) and IRAs and think that they have accomplished enough for you to retire. You need to do things wisely in today's economy. With the global economy, pandemics, stock market volatility, rising healthcare costs, and spiraling federal deficits, you need to educate yourself financially. It is best to consider your entire situation and plan holistically.

Some analysts talk about interest rates remaining low for quite some time, so where do we go to invest our safe money to get a reasonable rate of return?

Baby boomers are heading into retirement in droves, which is putting pressure on our social security system. People are living longer than ever, and many are concerned they are going to outlive their money. That is why we recommend people sit with an advisor who does complete and holistic planning.

You need to work with an advisor who is a fiduciary and has your best interest at stake—not just a registered representative who sells financial products.

When we plan for you, we create comprehensive financial plans that explore all areas of your finances:

- Taxes
- Healthcare costs
- Social security benefits
- Long-term care
- Legacy planning

We create a comprehensive plan that moves forward and is flexible enough to adjust to the changing economies, political wanes, and tax code.

About the Author

Donald Albach
President
Millstone Financial Group

Don has worked in the financial services industry for his entire professional career. Throughout every phase of Don's career, he has focused on retirement planning. From implementing small- to medium-sized company 401(k) Profit Sharing Plans to establishing an IRA for individual clients, Don has seen most aspects of the retirement planning process. Don's role at Millstone Financial Group is to work with clients to create Retirement Income Planning strategies that help guide them toward financial peace of mind.

Don graduated from Norwich University, "the nation's oldest private military college," in 1986. Upon graduation, Don went directly to work in New York City, joining First Boston's International Investment Group. From there, Don moved on to MetLife, where he spent the next eleven years working with employer group 401(k) plans. It was during this time that he realized while people were able to save for retirement, they had very little understanding of how to navigate the complexities of retirement. In 2013, Don decided to separate from MetLife and established Millstone Financial Group.

Don currently lives in Monroe Township, New Jersey, with his wife, Tina, to whom he has been married since 1992. They have three children together: Paige, Donny, and Ally. Don's two passions are sailing and watching college football. He also enjoys cooking Sunday dinner for his family.

How to Create a Rock-Solid Financial Plan That Will Stand the Test of Time

by Jamie Baraldi

In this day and age, people no longer work at companies for thirty or forty years as our parents may have. My father, a tugboat captain for over twenty years, unexpectedly lost his job when I was growing up, and we were forced to move. It had such a lasting impact on me, I wanted to make sure to develop a financial plan so that, as I grew older, I'd be in a secure position.

It has been said that most investors take more time planning a retirement trip than they do their retirement. This can cause problems at the worst time—during retirement. My mission has been to change that. Our mission is help people build comprehensive wealth management plans that will stand the test of time.

How to Create and Grow Your Wealth Over Time

When creating and growing wealth, analyze your investments with respect to all different categories that you are invested in, including:

- 401(k)s
- IRAs
- Taxable assets

List them all on one paper and review your list to make sure you have the appropriate investment mix. When we assist you in creating and growing your wealth, we also want to make sure you have adequate life insurance—what we term *life replacement strategies*. God forbid something should happen to you prior to reaching your goals. As always, we want to make sure as we grow your wealth that we are minimizing taxes on your investments. It is not how much you make; it is how much you keep.

To create and grow your wealth, follow a financial-planning-based approach:

1. Label your goals and dreams.

2. List your debts and obligations.

3. Name the time frame within which you would like to accomplish your goals and dreams.

4. Solve for what target rate of return do you need to attain those goals.

Once you establish these parameters, we work with you to find the safest way, or perhaps, the most conservative way, to reach that target rate of return. You have one life to live, and you want to live it the best way you can. So, plan your money around your life rather than your life around your money.

How to Protect and Preserve Your Wealth and Bullet-Proof Your Situation

In protecting and preserving your investments, you want to have your version of playing defense as well as being prepared for volatility. Analyze your overall investment plan. We want to determine your current *asset allocation management*. When you go through a financial planning process, you learn where you are today and what you will need to transition from point A—your current portfolio—to point B—where you want to be.

Scrutinize your *diversification management* to make sure you have an appropriate variety of investments. In playing defense and bullet-proofing your situation, you also want to examine your overall investment plan as it pertains to life, disability, long-term care, and liability planning. To bullet-proof your situation, make sure you have an adequate amount of coverage. Check with your financial advisor to affirm the amount and diversity of coverage is appropriate for your stage in life.

Lastly, make sure that your plan is cost effective. In preparing for volatility, think of the markets like the seasons: spring, summer, fall, and inevitably, winter, which would be a bear market. If you are properly positioned in this stage, you will be better equipped to weather that storm. As we know, spring returns after the winter, and that is when, if you are properly positioned, you can take advantage.

How to Plan for Distributions and Income Streams in Retirement

In planning for distributions of wealth during our lifetime and in retirement, we want to ensure you choose the most secure way to provide a consistent stream of income. Within qualified retirement plans, we find investment issues when transitioning from a growth-mode portfolio to a more income-generating portfolio. Consider the different buckets or baskets of assets you have, and create a distribution stream in the most tax-advantageous way. Once again, it's not how much you make, it's how much you keep.

To bullet-proof your situation, arrange a durable power of attorney so that if anything should happen to you, someone can act on your behalf. With the advent of the Roth IRA, you want to take a close look at transitioning assets from 401(k) s and IRAs, retirement accounts, converting assets over to a Roth IRA that will create a tax-free bucket in the future.

How to Prepare for Healthcare in Retirement

Another area to prepare for in retirement is healthcare. Here are some areas to explore; some require input from your financial advisor:

1. Are you current with medical check-ups and any procedures you need to have?

2. Do you have a corporate health plan? Compare how that will change in retirement with acquiring independent healthcare or other alternatives.

3. Have you researched long-term care? Make sure that you have a plan in place so that, should something happen to you, you do not become a burden to your loved ones. Long-term care is not an all-or-nothing option. You can partially insure yourself, which may be easier to afford and can reduce the need to hedge your bets against the risk of catastrophe.

4. Consider Medicare planning in anticipation of turning sixty-five. Because Medicare frequently changes its options, list any and all medications you take and any other Medicare needs you may have to determine which specific plan works best for your situation.

You want to work closely with your accountant or tax attorney while considering these issues.

Plan of Distributions at Death

An estate attorney is essential to help you with this plan.

You want to make sure you dot the I's and cross the T's, which includes:

- Proper titling of all of your assets

- Confirming the executor or trustee of your estate plan: are they still the person you want?

- Addressing continuity issues

- Allocating distributions of wealth to spouse, descendants, and others done in the most tax-efficient way

- Ensuring an adequate life insurance policy or, as we say, a *wealth replacement policy* is in place

- Retaining full control for whoever is going to manage the assets and pull funds to keep the plan intact—that means no unnecessary distributions, penalties, fees, or charges

Taking care of the estate planning ahead of time will relieve your loved ones of the burden of going through that process. If you do not have an estate plan and you do not have a will, your estate is considered to be *intestate,* which means the state becomes your executor. And we all know how difficult it can be working with the government during a difficult time.

We follow a set of steps to complete a comprehensive financial plan:

1. Establish goals.

2. Assess income needs.

3. Decide which cash flows will be needed.

4. Estimate the time horizon for each goal.

5. Estimate life expectancy.

While doing that, we negotiate the degree of risk or fluctuations you are willing to accept.

From there we move on to the strategy. You want what we call a *Three-Bucket Approach*:

1. In the first bucket are monies you might need for the next one-to-three years. They typically consist of stable investments, such as cash or short-term high-quality bonds.

2. In bucket two are monies you might need in the next, say, four-to-seven years. This is your core asset allocation: a blend of stocks, bonds, and alternatives.

3. The third bucket we call the *Inflation Bucket*. It is your long-term bucket—eight-plus years—used for higher growth to offset the cost of inflation.

Once you have followed these steps, it is time to implement the plan. Typically, you want to maintain 80 to 90 percent of your portfolio in what we call a *core portfolio* that should not change over time, with 10 to 20 percent of the portfolio more tactical and flexible in nature.

Once that is done, you need to be diligent in reviewing the portfolio on a consistent basis. We recommend a quarterly review to consider opportunities to rebalance the portfolio or reposition the portfolio to maintain the target allocation. Additionally, once a year, roll up your sleeves and review your overall financial plan.

Has anything changed?

Your goals, time horizons, risks, tolerance?

Has anything in your situation changed such that it would denote changing your financial plan, and therein your asset allocation in your portfolio?

It is our pleasure to serve those who need help in assessing their needs and resources for a comfortable, healthy retirement.

About the Author

Jamie Baraldi
Founder and CEO
Peak Wealth Partners

Jamie Baraldi is the founder and the CEO of Peak Wealth Partners. He has been a financial advisor for more than twenty-seven years, beginning at Dean Witter in 1993. Jamie has always had a passion for the financial field. He earned his BA in Economics and Finance at Muhlenberg College and later completed University of Pennsylvania's Executive Business Program. A lifelong learner, Jamie has earned the designation of Chartered Retirement Planning Counselor from the College of Financial Planning. He specializes in working with pre-retirees and retirees, providing comprehensive wealth management solutions and helping guide clients into and throughout retirement.

In his leisure, Jamie enjoys playing soccer, running, reading, spending time with family, and volunteering.

Getting Excited About the Possibilities of Your Assets in Retirement for You and Your Heirs

by John Davenport

Here at Davenport & Associates, Inc., we approach wealth planning like no other firm in the marketplace today. We focus on exploring the possibilities with assets in retirement rather than simply trying to sell an investment. One of the biggest compliments a client can give us is when they tell us we speak to them like no one has ever spoken to them before—not their broker, accountant, nor attorney.

We don't sell a client on an investment; rather, we use all different types of assets in retirement. I am not here as the Jim Cramer of the world; I am not trying to sell a client on the hot stock, or the hot mutual fund, of the day. I am a qualified professional who can look at every type of asset you have worked your entire life to build. Based upon the purpose and tax characteristics, I can advise you how to invest and position those assets for maximum income, transfer of wealth, and minimization of estate, income, and capital gain taxes. My unique wealth-planning methodology can work for you.

I want to help you be excited about what you have built. Everybody has a different asset mix. My goal is to teach you how to invest and position your assets for the same four-pronged purpose:

1. Maximize income

2. Maximize wealth transfer without any adverse impact on the quality of your retirement

3. Minimize or eliminate estate, income, or capital gain taxes

4. Direct *social capital*, i.e., tax dollars to causes of your choice and not the IRS

Believe it or not, you will come to do it all with more certainty and peace of mind than you have ever enjoyed in your financial life. I give clients who are in retirement or approaching retirement an understanding of how to use assets. If you work with my firm, the word frequently coming out of my mouth is *purpose*.

What is the purpose of that life insurance policy you bought twenty years ago?

What is the purpose of this brokerage investment account?

To really understand how to invest properly, you first must understand the purpose of the asset. Typically, people have done a marvelous job of accumulating a degree of wealth. But as they enter into retirement, they may not understand the extraction of the benefits of their wealth is an entirely different art form. What I want to do is expose my clients to this art form and the profound difference it can make in their own and their family's lives. And that is what I will help you understand.

It starts to be fun when I show you exciting possibilities, new ideas and strategies you may not have thought of before, for how to use these assets. They can make profound differences in both your own and your family's life. That is the part I enjoy. I like creating the vision for you of where we can go, what the tax benefits could be, what the income benefits could be, and so on.

We like putting you in the driver's seat, where you can choose when to retire. Retirement should be a question of choice, not of necessity. I should say *work* becomes the question of choice, not of necessity. I have a passion for what I do. I love what I do, and it is extremely satisfying to make a true qualitative difference in my clients' lives. By doing so, that usually translates into a long and comprehensive relationship with my clients.

You may think this sounds too good to be true. Well, we often get that response. But I used to work for a large law firm in New York City, and in working with very wealthy people, I found two things to be true:

1. Most people have never heard about the investment and tax strategies we expose our clients to. I am a big believer in people knowing all the rights and options for making the most of what they have worked so hard for their entire lives. Whether you follow our advice or not, when you work with our firm, it is not a question of convincing you to do something or to buy something. I sell a lot of investments and insurance products. That is not the issue. The issue is taking the time to understand how to make the most of it. If you are motivated to learn how to use your assets most effectively, I can show you how. That's right, I can help you. But I cannot motivate you.

2. Many people do not want to spend the time to learn. But, learning how to retire well doesn't require a major commitment of time. What makes my firm different is that we approach wealth planning in an entirely different way from anybody in the marketplace.

Some people are skeptical; they want to know if it's so successful, why isn't anyone else taking the same approach?

I say, "The reason is that they haven't met me yet."

I try to get in front of as many people and families as I can. Then I can impart some wisdom to them about what we do and how effectively we have been in doing it. Ours is a different approach, but it is a comfortable approach because we are not trying to sell you on a simple investment. Rather we strive to educate you, to excite you, to applaud you on the work that you have done, and to put a smile on your face while creating more certainty and peace of mind in retirement. Additionally, we want to witness you accomplish all the objectives we lay out for you. We are very proud of our track record.

Using Assets Based on Purpose and Taxation

Let me use an example. I will use assets that most clients own and depend upon for a comfortable retirement: IRAs and Qualified Plan assets.

By qualified plans, I mean:

- 401(k) plans
- 403(b) plans
- Tax-deferred annuities
- Nonqualified deferred compensation plans
- Assets that have never before been taxed, typically targeted toward your retirement

The goal when I work with a client with these pre-tax assets is to not die with the highest valued IRA or qualified-plan asset because these are the worst possible tax assets to die with. Most people do not understand that. Typically, if I am dealing with a married couple, I am talking about the death of the surviving spouse. After the death of the first spouse, monies like this typically will rollover to the surviving spouse. They will continue to take income, and then when they want to transfer them to a third party upon their death, for example, their children, that is when Uncle Sam rears his ugly head.

If you wait to take the required minimum distributions from these pre-tax assets at age seventy-two, you'll fall into what I have termed the *IRS Tax Trap*. I have written many articles and a chapter of another book, *The Wealth Maximization Method*, on this topic. To beat Uncle Sam at his own game, you must truly understand the purpose of these assets. The purpose is not to die with the highest amount of these assets, but rather to learn to use them while living to provide more income for you and more wealth transfer for your heirs.

I show you how to position and invest these assets in such a way that you can take income as a couple when you want it and how to retain more wealth transfer of these assets to your heirs. But by investing it for the purpose it was intended, which is *income*, you can take well in excess of the required minimum distribution at age seventy-two, when you want the income. Then, with the excess guaranteed income from these assets and other assets, third parties of the finest quality and strength will guarantee you and your spouse well in excess of the required minimum distribution at age seventy-two. And you can start that income when you want to, not when when the government tells you to.

We use a portion to create for you a new and more effective portfolio asset that I and other attorneys call the *IRA Trust*. The IRA Trust serves like a super-charged Roth IRA for you, without requiring you to pay tax on it. In this way, you receive more from a wealth transfer asset when you want it, and not when the government tells you to take it. This means you can move more tax-free wealth from these assets to your heirs than you ever would have if you had never met me. This way you win, your heirs win, and the IRS loses.

Maximizing Income

If I could send you home with a bumper sticker that would encapsulate how we approach wealth planning like no other firm, that bumper sticker would read:

INCOME CREATES POSSIBILITIES

The driving force in our methodology is to find ways of generating maximum income by positioning all your assets to accomplish the same four objectives. So, we create a cohesive purpose from what is typically an unstructured and non-purposeful accumulation of assets.

We create this cohesive purpose with the same four objectives:

1. Maximize income for you and your spouse and the tax efficiency of that income.

2. Maximize the transfer of wealth to your heirs without any adverse impact on the quality of your own retirement.

3. Minimize or eliminate estate taxes, income taxes, and capital gains taxes.

4. Redirect *social capital dollars*—any ultimate tax dollars that might be due on your estate—to causes of your choice, as opposed to sending it off to the IRS to be redistributed any which way they want.

We do it all, believe it or not, with more certainty and peace of mind than you have yet to enjoy in your financial life. That is how we like to show our clients to do it. And once again, the driving force here is maximizing your income.

If the planning is done properly, my clients typically take more than two times what the government requires them to take from IRAs and qualified plans well before the required minimum distribution age of seventy-two. Some of my clients take income from IRAs and qualified plans as early as their late fifties and early sixties. The income is guaranteed for life from the best third parties in the world.

If we can generate more income for you, it provides you other planning opportunities. You could use the excess income to spend, gift, or reinvest for your heirs. The main goal is to get it out of your IRAs and qualified plans.

Most affluent families in the world have irrevocable trusts, like the *IRA Trust*, funded with joint life insurance. This insurance pays the proceeds at the death of the last surviving spouse. By insuring two lives rather than one, you can maximize the death benefit, which is precisely the reason for creating the trust. We use the excess income from your IRAs and qualified plans together with excess income from other types of assets to fund these trusts. For example, you can use those excess dollars after you pay taxes at your lower effective tax rate and place it more effectively inside a trust outside of the estate totally tax free.

Clients are very insurable well into their eighties. A couple at seventy years old would typically pay approximately $10,000 per million for permanent life insurance. What investment does a retired couple have that would allow them to invest $10,000 today and be worth $1 million tax free tomorrow? The answer is none. The IRA Trust will be the best wealth transfer investment the client will ever have for their heirs.

Not only do we show you how to generate more guaranteed income from your income-producing assets, we also show you how to use a portion of excess income from your assets to transfer more wealth than perhaps you would have ever made in the marketplace alone, and you never have to worry about it. Having accomplished what I've described, you can go off and do all the wonderful things you have always wanted to do. And that makes for a very good and comprehensive relationship with our clients.

Maximizing Wealth Transfer for Your Heirs

What assets are more tax favorable for the client's heirs to inherit?

Certainly, IRAs and pre-tax assets are not the assets of choice to leave to your heirs. The assets of choice to leave to your heirs are what I like to call *wealth transfer trusts.*

There are many names that attorneys like me use for these trusts such as:

- IRA Trusts
- Wealth Enhancement Trusts
- Wealth Replacement Trusts
- Life Insurance Trusts

I like to call it an *IRA trust* when using the client's IRAs and pre-tax assets more effectively for income while replacing them more tax efficiently for their heirs. The heirs love to inherit these trusts because these assets are pure cash to them, payable within two or three weeks of the death of the last surviving spouse. We always want to maximize the wealth transfer only as a secondary thing. In other words, we are not going to ask a client to sacrifice the quality of their retirement by spending their hard-earned dollars in making their heirs richer, but rather using some of their excess income that they otherwise would have reinvested back into a bad tax asset to create a better tax asset for their heirs to inherit.

The more income I can produce for you above and beyond what you may need, the more options you will have for using your funds more effectively.

So, what are those other options?

Gift excess income. Gifts can be made in two ways. You can gift it as a living gift; there are limitations to that every year. Or, you can make what are called *testamentary gifts.* Testamentary gifts are gifts in trust for the children, payable at the death of the last surviving spouse. These gifts can actually be leveraged significantly tax free. So, they are a very effective tool.

Reinvest excess income. You can reinvest your excess income into something that is a bit more of a tax advantage for the children to inherit, like a *brokerage account,* funded with stocks or something like that, as a pure growth investment. It is a great asset for the children to inherit.

Create more wealth for your heirs. If you cannot use all the income we create for you in retirement, rather than put it back into a bad tax asset, like an IRA, I can show you how to use that to create more wealth for your heirs. You do not have to worry about it. These are dollars that your children ultimately would have been taxed on by Uncle Sam at your death anyway.

So, the only loser in this game is Uncle Sam. You have more income when you want it and you're healthy enough to use it. The heirs have more wealth than you ever would have been able to make in the marketplace alone, and the only loser in the game is Uncle Sam.

Direct Social Capital Dollars/Taxes Where You, Not the IRS, Choose

When asked, many clients think having a charitable intent means giving their money away. But if I asked you to put down on a piece a paper a charity that you would rather send your tax dollars to, could you come up with an entity other than the IRS? You probably could—it's a pretty easy exercise, right? What we are talking about here are tax dollars.

If there are ways of avoiding different types of taxes and directing those taxes to causes of your choice, wouldn't you prefer that?

Obviously, this results in more control for you. In our trademark programs, we show our clients how to do this.

Charitable contributions are a direct result of a lot of the investment strategies we show our clients. Let's consider *highly appreciated assets*.

Highly appreciated assets are the client's winners, such as:

- Highly appreciated stocks
- Highly appreciated real estate
- Anything you want to avoid selling so you do not have to pay the capital gains tax

The most commonly used method for avoiding capital gain on the sale of a highly appreciated asset—not the most effective, mind you—is what I like to call the *Death Method.*

How does the Death Method work?

Let's suppose I have a stock that I bought thirty years ago for $20,000 that's now worth $500,000. If I were to die and leave that stock to my son, my son would receive an increase, or, in accounting parlance, a *step-up* in the purchase price of that asset to the value of that asset as of the day of my death. So, if my son turned around the very next day after I died and decided to sell that stock—and obviously the mourning period was very short—then my son would pay nothing in capital gains tax.

Well, that is great for my son, but it does not do very much for me. You can benefit directly in the form of income by using a charitable remainder trust effectively as part of your retirement planning.

The steps for this strategy are as follows:

1. Contribute highly appreciated assets into a charitable trust.

2. Sell it within the trust.

3. Generate significant levels of income. In the stock I was selling in my example above, the income would be almost four times the dividend income. There

would be significant income tax deductions based on the residual gift to charity.

4. Use some of the tax savings to actually replace the value of that asset to the heirs, with joint life insurance, outside the estate, totally tax free.

So, you would now have more income, when you want it, when you are healthy enough to use it, and when you and your spouse are still together to use it.

You would not have to pay the capital gains tax. You'd get significant income tax deductions off of that income, making that income for the first five or six years virtually tax free. Some of the excess monies or some of the tax savings would be used to get Uncle Sam to subsidize the replacement of that gift to the heirs tax free.

Meanwhile, you would be able to direct where those ultimate tax dollars go after you and your spouse have passed on. You'd get to name charities of your choice, and you would be able to control the asset, maximize the income, replace the asset tax free to your heirs and, at the same time, make a social capital gift to the cause of your choice rather than simply sending it off to the IRS to be redistributed in any which way they want. That is the social capital concept.

This is a very effective and well-recognized tool. You control the entire situation and enjoy all the benefits. That's an effective *usage* strategy with significant qualitative benefits to you and your family.

Create More Peace of Mind and Certainty in Retirement Than Ever Before

When we work with our clients, we find one of their biggest concerns is running out of income in retirement. But if I do my job properly—achieving those four objectives: 1) maximize income, 2) maximize the transfer of wealth, 3) minimize tax, and 4) direct social capital and create more certainty and peace of mind—then the income we generate for you will be guaranteed by the best third parties in the world. Now, that income can still increase each year, but it cannot decrease regardless of actual market performance. It's like creating a pension for you, a pension that can only go up. So, you don't have to worry about it.

The income we can produce is far in excess of that which you may have been producing prior to you coming to work with us. My clients transfer more wealth to their children than they ever would have made simply in the marketplace alone. We replace and enhance the wealth transfer to the heirs outside their estate for tax purposes through the use of trusts, life insurance, and things of this nature. They enjoy the peace of mind, knowing that even if they were to go through every dime of their own assets—spend the last one of those dollars on the last day of the last survivor's death—

their heirs are still going to get the life insurance proceeds inside their trust, tax free.

The proper planning basically takes the heirs out of the equation, so the client can focus on the use of their assets for the *income* they worked so hard for and from which they benefit directly. If we can protect and maximize the income for the client while creating more tax-free wealth for the client's heirs, all with greater certainty and peace of mind, then we have done well for our clients. Through our trademarked programs, the clients enjoy more guaranteed income, more wealth transfer, and more peace of mind than they ever enjoyed in their financial lives.

Is this a different approach to wealth planning?

Without a doubt, but it is one that produces great qualitative benefit to the client and their heirs. Our clients have come back to tell us it works, which we take great pride in knowing. But it also creates a very comprehensive and lifelong relationship with my clients. I have never lost a client to any of my three trademark programs. And again, it is not because I am trying to sell them the hot stock or the hot mutual fund of the day. It's because I have shown them a different approach that provides more certainty of income and more certainty of wealth transfer, so that they can go off and enjoy a very comfortable and peaceful retirement.

That is a wonderful result of our planning and a great compliment to our firm.

About the Author

John Davenport
President
Davenport & Associates

John Davenport is President of Davenport & Associates and the creator of the Wealth Maximization Method. John works closely with his clients to prepare for and successfully manage their retirement.

Prior to the founding of Davenport & Associates, John served as a corporate officer for TIAA-CREF, which is the largest pension investment company in the world. He also worked as an estate and trust attorney for a large estate planning firm in New York, and as an Executive Vice President and Wealth Planner for Merrill Lynch in the wealth planning area.

He received his undergraduate degree from the University of Notre Dame, his MBA in Finance from Fordham University, and his law degree from Pace University. John's professional licenses include FINRA Series 6, 7, 63, and 65, making him a fully licensed securities broker and an agent of a Registered Investment Advisor. John is also a fully licensed insurance broker, as well as a licensed attorney in the states of New York and Connecticut.

Surviving in Today's New Economy

by Grant Dorhout

The only thing that has been consistent is change. Our world is a rapidly changing environment economically and financially. Surviving this economy can become extraordinarily confusing because who knows which way the wind is blowing? I hope discussing these few topics will help you better understand whether you need additional help or you are positioned properly for the coming years. You may be in the early stages of your investing, in the middle of it, or nearing or in retirement. I hope to help you navigate an extremely confusing world and give you confidence in moving forward.

To survive today's new economy, you have to make sure your information comes from a reliable, trustworthy source. Take into consideration all aspects of your finances. How you think can impact other areas. For example, politics can influence tax laws or other legislation that may impact you negatively. These other factors can change how well you are positioned for the future.

You need to plan properly to progress in any area of your life. It does not stop at finance. If you fail to plan, you plan to fail, as the saying goes, and that is what I firmly believe. Your planning must incorporate many viewpoints. If you do not keep a broad view while planning, there will likely be a huge hole in your financial life. It might be early on or in the middle of your life; it might be just as you begin your retirement. It may be a big surprise, perhaps something you could have planned your way out of to get you through retirement in a better way.

Listening to the Right Informational Source

All too often, people come to me with information they got from Facebook, or maybe they watch one of the major news outlets, whether it's a conservative or liberal source—it doesn't matter which. They take the opinions of someone on social media or on any type of virtual platform, and they take it as gospel truth. The same financial faith can be misplaced in certain news anchors. It is clear that these sources express their own opinions, to which they are totally entitled; however, an opinion is not fact.

What reference is the Facebook user or news anchor using?

If you are doing your own research, make sure that you consult appropriate and credible sources. If it is a health issue, use the Centers for Disease Control and Prevention (CDC). Find out what the CDC actually says about that particular topic. Regarding politics, don't settle for just one person's opinion. Follow up with sound research, and check with your local representatives to find out what they actually say. There are plenty of resources to consult for the information you need. If you're seeking financial advice, do not just take someone's opinion on Facebook and believe it is good enough. For finances, you want to find a good independent fiduciary advisor to consult as you move forward on those topics.

How Politics Influence Finances

Opinions, motivations, and passions stem from political beliefs or what a person's perceived political beliefs are. Know what you believe politically and *why* you believe it. Try to avoid being a single-item voter. It does not matter what the single item is—if you focus on only one issue, you may be ignoring whether your ideals match the ideals of the party you vote for. You need to reassess why you believe what you believe. Representatives, senators, and state and local governments are vying for your vote. They are trying to motivate you politically, and they may be motivating you politically to vote in a way that is contrary to your beliefs.

So, make sure you are asking yourself: *Why do I believe what I believe?*

Those politicians could enact laws that can adversely affect what you believe from a holistic standpoint. They could make changes that affect your finances and retirement plans.

Your Tax Future

Our debt is ballooning—ballooning beyond where we ever thought it could expand. Politicians tell us that they are the ones who will balance the budget, but we are $26 trillion dollars in national debt. That number continues to rise at approximately $1 million dollars every twenty seconds. That is a very scary thing! It's important to note, however, that this figure for our national debt does not include unfunded liabilities. Unfunded liabilities are many times this amount. It would scare most of us to know the exact dollar amount. This figure increases so rapidly, it is hard to keep track.

So, here we are, in a situation in which the government can do one of two things to balance its budget or to get on the right track: Either they must spend less or they can make more. They have proven over the last many years that spending less is not going to happen. It is the same for you and me in our households—we can either spend less or make more to balance our finances. Our government only can do that by spending less or making more.

The only way our government can make more money is by increasing tax revenue, which means increasing your taxes. How are you positioned for taxes? At some point we will have higher tax rates than we do at this point.

When doing proper tax planning, you need to take into consideration:

- What your tax past has been
- What the likelihood is in the future
- Current tax laws

In 1944, the United States levied our highest marginal tax rate at 94 percent. After that, it went down steadily, and now, in the year 2020, the top marginal tax rate is 37 percent. Now, a lot of people are not in the top marginal tax rates, but it has become a more favorable tax treatment. If the rate increases in the future, it may make sense to move any tax deferred wealth, meaning 401(k)s and 403(b)s, into a more tax-free environment. This could be a Roth IRA, a Roth 401(k), municipal bonds, or cash value life insurance. These would all be viable options to utilize for your future, from a tax perspective only.

Focus on the Facts

It may be tempting to take the advice of a friend who says, "I just bought this brand-new, perfect, *whatever* investment and it is going to satisfy all of my needs."

We take that as the truth because we trust them. Although they may be trustworthy in general, they may not be qualified to give that financial information to you. Therein lies the problem. There is no perfect investment. However, it is possible to put together a package of investments that could be a near-perfect plan.

It's a common misconception that there's a perfect mutual fund that will be the best retirement plan. Well, a retirement plan involves a great income plan, and a mutual fund at its core is designed to grow. It is not designed for a great income source.

If you need a great income source, you would look to something more like:

- Annuities
- Life insurance policies
- A pension-like plan that can bring in more reliable income

If you want to grow, look to stocks, exchange-traded funds (ETFs), and mutual funds. Every single investment, every single product, was built for a specific reason. You need to learn the specific reason that product was developed, and make sure the way you are using it is actually what it was intended for. As an example, I have two vehicles. One of them is an SUV; one of them is a pickup. The pickup is designed to pull my camper; the SUV is not designed to pull my camper. If I try to pull my camper with my SUV, it can have catastrophic consequences. If you try to utilize financial products in a way they are not designed, it will have catastrophic consequences to your financial future.

Positioning

Consider your risk tolerance. Ask yourself:

- *What is my need for this money?*
- *When do I need it?*
- *How do I want to have this ride?*

No matter your age right now, think about how you want the ride of your money to be. Do you want it to be smooth?

That tells you a lot about how you need to position yourself financially. If you want it to be relatively smooth, you do not want to be invested solely in stocks, because that is going to be a bumpy ride—kind of like driving down a dirt road in the country.

If you want a smooth ride, like going down the highway, you want to be more balanced, meaning you want to have more secured assets. You want to utilize certain annuities that will limit losses. You may go into select ETFs with certain loss parameters that will not allow you to lose so much. If you are willing to go down that bumpy road, and you want to experience the really high highs and the really low lows, that is okay. There is nothing wrong with that. Then, you are going to want to be in more stock positions or possibly ETFs positions, and take those loss parameters off.

You may want to employ more of a balancing strategy, wherein if certain asset classes are depressed at a certain time, you rebalance and buy them at a lower value. If you are in the early stages of your life, you may shift more toward stocks. If you are in the later stages, nearing or in retirement, then you would do well to start looking at more income-bearing products, not taking on so much risk.

If you do not have a pension, a 401(k), 403(b), 457, or any retirement plan, your challenge is to convert them into a reliable income source that looks like a pension. Start using investments like annuities for this purpose because that is what they were designed for. Do not put all your eggs in any one basket, because, like I said before and I will say again, there is no perfect product, but there could be a perfect package of products to create a nearly perfect plan for whatever your goal is.

About the Author

Grant Dorhout
Founder and President
Dorhout Retirement Services

Grant is the founder and president of Dorhout Retirement Services located in Omaha, Nebraska. He has been helping his clients retire with confidence since 2005. His approach is one that puts the focus on making sure everyone he works with has a plan that works in all circumstances, not just ideal ones.

Even with his extensive experience, Grant strives to continuously educate himself on the tools and resources that could create positive impact for his clients. By constantly seeking out cutting-edge solutions, Grant provides his clients with a variety of financial options resulting in a truly unique retirement plan. Every decision Grant and his clients make together will have the most powerful potential impact possible; both here and now, and for generations to come.

Grant and his wife, Erika, and their three wonderful children, are heavily involved in their Omaha community. They love spending time outdoors and creating new memories together.

A Well-Defined Retirement Income Plan

by Rick Durkee

The importance of a well-defined retirement income plan is like a sailboat on the ocean: If you want to get somewhere, you've got to have a rudder, or a mechanism to steer your course. If you do not have a plan in place before it is your time to retire, how can you chart a course properly and navigate the different risks, issues, and opportunities that will occur during the twenty-year, thirty-year, or longer retirement?

I liken myself to a train conductor—I can pick you up and help you get where you want to be. I have more than twenty years of experience navigating the territory. But it's up to you to hop on board. Are you ready?

Your Process Is Tied to Your Success

I want you to put yourself back in the time when you were learning to do what you do. How did you learn to become successful at your work?

Answering these questions will help prompt your memory:

- Did you receive additional education to be able to continue in your career?

- Did you learn experientially, i.e., learn by doing?

- Were you mentored by someone?

- Did you learn by following a step-by-step process?

Over the last twenty-plus years of working with individuals on retirement planning, we have found that those who followed a process in their working careers were much more successful aligning with how we at the Coastal Financial Planning Group make proper financial decisions regarding your retirement. A surgeon must carefully follow a well-defined process to achieve a successful surgery. An architect must draft a set of comprehensive building plans well in advance of ordering materials or starting construction. All the clients we've advised who are accustomed to following a process in their working lives have found that applying those same principles help them easily develop their plan to achieve their retirement goals. Retirement planning is much more effective when you accept that following a process is necessary. We are here to help you define and follow that process.

Ask the Right Questions to Find the Solution You Seek

Many clients come to us having been successful in their work, but feeling at a loss to plan effectively for retirement. They don't know where to begin, but they are eager to follow our lead. A woman recently reached out to us on the internet, explaining she was part of the airline industry's mass retirement offered recently due to the COVID-19 situation.

"I don't know what questions to ask," she said. "I just do not know where to begin."

I explained to her that we use a simple three-step financial review process. I introduced the steps to her briefly and said we could move on to the next step after that day's meeting. She was accepting of our process because she did not have a method of getting the information she needed. She knew that in order to achieve a successful retirement, she would be called on to make critical retirement decisions that needed to be based on facts and logic instead of myths, misconceptions, and incomplete information.

Retirement decisions are often like squeezing toothpaste out of the tube; when you squeeze the tube, you cannot put the toothpaste back in. We need to get the proper information up front to make these critical financial decisions that often cannot be reversed.

ISO Accreditation for a Business

Many people coming from the manufacturing industry understand the International Standards Organization (ISO). ISO provides an evaluation tool that examines the risks, issues, and opportunities facing a business. At the Coastal Financial Planning Group, we evaluate the same risks, issues, and opportunities facing retirees. We annually review all our procedures and audit them both internally and externally to maintain our ISO accreditation. Simply stated, having our ISO accreditation at the Coastal Financial Planning Group ensures that we say what we do and do what we say.

No other independent group firm in financial services has it. In addition to our process, we have a certified financial planner on staff, and we feel this combination allows us to cultivate what we call *procedural trust* with our current and potential clients. If we are handling someone's life savings as they move into retirement, we owe it to them to have a well-defined process for their retirement income plans. Creating procedural trust is key because, in the financial service industry, this trust is necessary to give people confidence they have chosen the right person or firm to handle their life savings.

If we are handling someone's life savings as they move into retirement, we owe it to them to have our procedures well documented. Our accreditation process took almost five years, and we have had the accreditation for four years now. Procedural trust is the key. In the financial services industry, you have to create procedural trust if you want to give people the confidence that you are the right person or firm to handle their life savings.

Define Outcome Investing

What if you could define your investment results and feel confident they were achievable within the amount of risk you are willing to take?

Defined outcome investing allows you to earmark assets to create income based on parameters set for risk and, in turn, give a higher probability for success in meeting your goals for growth in retirement. There are two methods of defined outcome investing:

1. **Growth investing.** When you are investing in your pre-retirement years, you want to make sure to focus on growth investing. Growth investing is an accumulation vehicle. It typically means you are willing to take more risks because you have a longer time horizon before you plan to use your money.

2. **Income investing.** However, in your retirement years, a shift occurs from accumulation or growth of your wealth to a spend-down of your retirement assets. During this period, risk is reduced to achieve the desired income of a well-defined retirement income plan.

Transitioning from growth investing to income investing during the retirement red zone, or the five to ten years prior to and the five to ten years after retirement, is critical to increase the probability of a successful retirement where assets don't run out before you do! Having this well-defined retirement income plan can also reduce market risk and longevity risk along with sequence of returns risk. These are all risks we have faced any time markets have dropped significantly, and we are withdrawing from our investments to create retirement income.

Defined Income Planning

Remember the analogy that I used in the beginning of this chapter, the sailboat without a rudder?

Developing a retirement income plan *before* you develop strategies of how you want to invest will help you increase your odds for a successful retirement.

If you do not have the navigation plan in place, how can you possibly know which investments to steer toward to accomplish your goals?

A well-defined retirement income plan will incorporate your expenses, your sources of income, and your time frame of how long those assets should last.

This means we can avoid the number one fear of all retirees: *Will my money last as long as I need it to?*

A well-known financial author named Anthony Robbins says, "Old and broke are two things I do not want to experience at the same time in retirement."

Defined income planning, using a well-defined process, can help you avoid that number one risk retirees face. At the

Coastal Financial Planning Group, we assist you in creating your well-defined retirement income plan before we make any financial decisions about investments. This way, your retirement income plan will be best suited to achieve your retirement income goals, and you will have followed a well-defined process that uses the facts and logic you learned during your process of discovery.

Discover your course to navigate into and through your retirement!

About the Author

Rick Durkee
President and Chief Investment Advisor
Coastal Financial Planning Group

As the Founder and President of the Coastal Financial Planning Group, Rick Durkee is a recognized leader of the financial services industry in Charleston, South Carolina. Since founding the Coastal Financial Planning Group in 2003, he has served his clients and community by offering advanced retirement planning solutions for individuals and business owners.

Rick earned his reputation as a strategist in retirement planning and asset management by adopting an approach called *income allocation,* a financial planning concept that focuses on developing a written retirement income plan to address any income shortfalls that may occur in one's retirement lifespan, while avoiding the biggest risks in retirement, including longevity risk, market risk, and market sequence of returns risk.

Prior to opening his doors at the Coastal Financial Planning Group, Rick developed his passion as a retirement advisor with recognized investment and insurance firms such as Prudential, New York Life, and MetLife, where he earned his designation as a Life Underwriting Training Council Fellow, LUTCF. His core values for helping people understand their retirement needs and the kind of planning required for meeting those goals are apparent to the listeners of his two informative podcasts that broadcast worldwide and are available on the website CFPGroup.biz, *Navigating Retirement* and *Christian Business Values*.

Rick is an ambassador for the South Carolina Christian Chamber of Commerce. He earned his bachelor's degree in business management and marketing from the University of South Carolina in 1981. Professionally, he holds a Series 65 securities license, as well as the Life, Health, and Disability insurance license for South Carolina and several other states in which he serves his clients. He and his wife, Violet, have lived in West Ashley for the last twenty years.

The Firm With a Different Approach

by Billy Evans

Everything about the way I entered the investment management field and how I created my firm was different—from the very beginning.

I don't get bogged down in details; I want to spend all my time helping clients. The approach is not something you will find elsewhere, to my knowledge. It makes our firm distinctive—and successful.

I'm Billy Evans, head of Evans Financial Services based in Marion, Virginia. My firm consists of four friendly support staff and myself.

Consider what makes Evans Financial Services distinctive:

My Background

I grew up on a cattle farm in southwestern Virginia, and my family owned a wholesale beer and wine distributorship. (That made me quite popular in high school for about six weeks until the kids realized I could not show up at parties with ten cases of beer). I had been interested in finances and planning but suddenly I inherited the process and details of selling the family business and investing the proceeds. That evolved into a career path with an industry veteran becoming my mentor.

My Timing

I opened in 2008 during the Great Recession. People were fearful, even panicking. The task at hand was to calm them down and to reduce the volatility decimating their portfolios.

My Business Model

I wanted to spend my time helping and educating clients and creating customized portfolios for them—portfolios based on their needs and risk tolerance, designed to meet their goals in good times and bad. I found a Registered Investment Advisor who shares my philosophies and takes the compliance specifics off my plate, leaving me more time to spend with my clients. I researched many portfolio managers, talked with them and narrowed down to about one dozen whom I liked. They used a tactical investment style I feel is important in portfolio management. I am constantly monitoring them, and their strategies, and I keep abreast of new managers who come along. It's amazing what one man can accomplish starting with a blank canvas and not being bound by any "we've always done it this way" constraints.

Baby boomers (those born between 1946 and 1965) are the bulk of our client base. They are at two stages: the ones pondering retirement and wondering if they can afford to, and the ones having made the decision and wanting a game plan.

Those who come in for preretirement interviews often walk out with something they did not expect. The interview is a good opportunity for us to create a plan for when they do retire. Some joke about being just one bad day away from choosing retirement, so most need several scenarios to choose from, and different routes to take if life change. We have found that after we have done the planning, we often can tell them that with their lifestyle they can retire next year. Yet, these people often end up working two, three, or four years longer than they planned. We have given them peace of mind. They can work because they want to, not because they have to. It takes the stress out of their situation.

Of course, some have not saved enough to retire. We tell them they may have to work a year or two longer than anticipated. Or, they may consider maximizing the income potential within their plan or making a change in their lifestyle and retirement spending.

Boomers who already have decided to retire go through a two-step fact-finding and interview process similar to the norm. We don't have an account minimum—I have a hard time saying no to someone in need—but the bulk of our clients have $400,000 to $600,000 in assets up to a couple of million.

The interview process and the emphasis on their goals and their risk tolerance are close to the norm. As for the products we choose and as for conforming to established formulas—well, there we go again, being different.

You've probably heard that portfolios should be split between so much bonds, so much stocks, and adjust the proportion as you age. The standard thinking is that different asset classes, say bonds and stocks, may move in different directions or with varying intensity as the economic cycles change. We have concluded from our research, however, that in times of severe economic stress, say the twelve to fifteen months around the dot-com crash in 2001 and the Great Recession in 2008, bonds have not been the safe haven everyone expected. Bondholders suffered too.

As a matter of fact, bonds may not be our first choice among fixed-income products, but that is a separate conversation.

We educate clients that the conventional wisdom of holding certain assets through good times and bad may not be the best course for them. Baby boomers, you see, are going to be the first generation to live statistically twenty to thirty years in retirement. Some may actually spend more years in retirement than they worked. Clients want to know if they will have enough money to last through retirement. A simple flash test that some advocate is to take a figure, say 80 percent of their current income, and see if a retirement portfolio can be created to match or exceed that level.

We get to that number in a different way. We ask clients about what they are spending their money on and their sources of income. We are trying to pin down how much money they need month to month. Does the plan meet their risk tolerance? Will they have the core cash they need and a way to get funds for emergencies? We don't want them to have to change their lifestyle just because of finances.

As I mentioned, boomers will be spending decades in retirement. By the time they quit working, many have paid off the house and their cars. But when you look at the prospect of living for another twenty-five or thirty years, you are going to be buying replacement cars, you are going to face home repair or remodeling bills. Not to mention travel expenses when you have the freedom to go where and when you want. Statistically, we know that people will spend a lot more money annually from sixty-five to seventy-five, the go-go years, than they will from seventy-five to eighty, the slow-go years.

By now, you know that I want to spend my time with clients, not tending to details and distractions. That is why I came up with the concept of using portfolio managers to handle client accounts according to strategies—usually rule-based strategies—that are flexible enough to adjust if markets take a sharp downturn.

Here's how the process works.

I favor eight to ten strategies of the hundreds available. Often the managers we use already have created a rule-based system. Sometimes there are algorithms involved in the system.

The analogy I use is that we operate like a nurse or doctor in a hospital, checking the patient's vital signs constantly. So, we are simply checking the vitals of the securities we hold versus the whole market daily. Most days there is nothing to change. But we check anyway.

When interviewing a prospective manager, I look at how they performed in the past when the wheels fell off the bus. Typically, they did not lose nearly as much money as the market.

And that's why our firm is using them now.

I do due diligence and basically stress test the manager's performance style. Later, if a new strategy comes along that I like, we may embrace it to make the overall portfolio stronger.

These managers handle the securities side of the market. Which brings us to the fixed-income side.

I like bond alternative vehicles where the principal is protected, preferably ones without fees. I do not consider a vehicle *safe* or *safer* unless it is guaranteed. The guarantees I want are from a third party. I want more than just the backing of the bank or institution issuing the product. Recall that in the Great Recession one large institution went under and others were forced into marriages with healthier partners.

We believe that our policy takes away some of the full-blown market risk. In addition, we believe that the way we manage securities takes away additional market risk. What are some of the products we use? Certificates of deposit guaranteed by a third party. Some insurance products meet that standard.

We use two of the five types of annuities. We use a straight fixed annuity that works basically like a certificate of deposit, but the money and the interest are deferred from taxes and there is seldom a big fee or payment associated with that. We use market-linked certificates of deposit, and fixed index annuities, and we are constantly looking for the best opportunities for clients from high-rated companies. You can have those products and not pay a fee.

I feel like the industry as a whole has a bad taste in its mouth from anything that smells like an annuity. That's because of the variable annuities popular in the nineties and early 2000s. The high fees involved really benefitted the sellers of the products, not the clients.

You will notice that I did not fall into the trap of saying the fixed-income side should be a certain percentage of the overall portfolio. That varies with the client, depending upon their income needs and especially their risk tolerance.

There is a concept in the industry known as sequence of returns risk. Meaning that if you retire and put most of your money into stocks just before the market tanks—say 2008—you are in trouble and may spend years trying to claw your way back. If you put money in just before a bull run—say 2012—and especially if you diversify, you should do well.

I have included a chart of some mathematical trickery. If you suffer a decline in your portfolio, maybe a drop from $300,000 to $150,000, that is a loss of 50 percent. But to climb back from $150,000 to your original $300,000 is a gain of 100 percent.

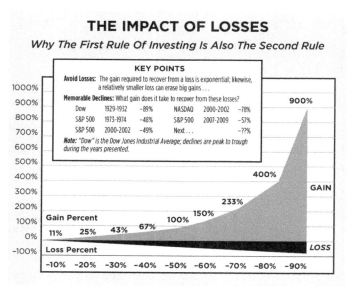

© Crestmont, used by permission

Trickery? Well, it is certainly counter-intuitive. The same amount of money but the drop is 50 percent while the gain required to climb back is 100 percent.

The best approach is to try to avoid that drop in the first place.

Recall that I opened my firm in 2008, hardly an auspicious time. I'm well acquainted with sequence of returns and the importance of avoiding that trap.

If I have done my job properly—perhaps leaving some chips on the table in the form of cash, perhaps investing in stages, perhaps recognizing that ominous times call for a greater amount of guaranteed fixed-income investments—the sequence of returns risk may be reduced.

Retirement planning is about more than money, it is about people.

In my highly nonscientific observations, people who say they are going to just lounge around the house in retirement tend not to live as long as those who have a passion, be it a hobby, volunteering, travel, or seeing the grandkids. It is not my role to be a life coach, but I do ask some diplomatic questions about their plans.

People come to retirement with widely varying levels of financial understanding. We spend quite a bit of time early on educating. We want them to know about mutual funds or exchange-traded funds (ETFs). We want them to grasp what we are recommending and why.

To that end, we hold educational seminars in addition to one-on-one sessions.

If they are struggling with the ins and outs of Medicare and Medi-gap coverage, we have a specialist to help them.

One of the things clients like about our approach, I've learned via referrals, is they typically never feel rushed. They don't feel pressure.

We try to hold the client's hand, so to speak, to help them, to educate them, and assist them in evaluating their market tolerance and making decisions for their financial future. This means that we sometimes need more than the typical two meetings to develop a plan or scenarios that they feel confident with moving forward.

About the Author

Billy Evans
Founder and CEO
Evans Financial Services

Billy Evans is founder and CEO of Evans Financial Services. He spends weekends with the family on the cattle farm he grew up on and helps his father with the hard manual labor. Once a year, clients are invited to an appreciation event on the farm to experience a piece of Billy's life and be a part of the family.

~

Investment advisory services offered through Capital Advisor Network, LLC (CAN), an Indiana registered investment advisor. CAN and Evans Financial Services are independent of each other. Insurance products and services are not offered through CAN but are offered and sold through individually licensed and appointed agents.

Retirement Planning
With Some Special Touches
by Bryan Foster and Carol Carroll

We're different.

Some in the industry call us weird.

Yes, like the ugly duckling was weird in the beginning.

What we are is a son/mother firm. One that shows how to close the income gap in retirement, sometimes with a unique three buckets of income approach. We help clients traverse the Medicare supplement jungle and choose the policy that is best for them. (Yes, in this jungle cheapest is best and we can find that at lightning speed.) We go to meet clients on their turf—home, office or out amid the crops. We tell countless baby boomers they need to put themselves and their needs ahead of the kids and grandkids. (We show them an easy way to take the legacy issue off their shoulders. And we push them to go out and start having fun in retirement.)

Mom, with the alliterative name, has been in the business for thirty years and ventured on her own in 1998. She's the senior vice president now. Son Bryan, CEO, graduated from the Ohio State University—yes, he's a great football fan—and was on his way toward a career as a cardiologist. It wasn't the right fit, however, and in his heart he knew that the financial business had always been in his blood.

They may seem like two dramatically different fields but both help people with their quality of life, Bryan says. The transition was easy. It's helping someone with everything they ever worked for and everything they ever saved for their entire financial life.

BFFinancial is an independent firm, backed with the database resources of TD Ameritrade and some technology of its own.

We have the tools and the algorithms and the programs and all the new technology. Mom is old school leaning hard on the human factor; son is very much technology. We find that when there is a blend of the two, that really is the secret sauce. That's what makes clients happy.

Here are our approaches to some retirement aspects that make us stand out.

Closing the Income Gap in Retirement

Setting up an income for life and what they get depends upon the product you are writing for them. You know the size of the gap you have to close. So typically the solution is going to be an indexed annuity. We're going to look at one that doesn't have any fees. We're going to look at one that has a nice big bonus to increase the income base so that way they're getting extra money in their account, and there's even one right now that we particularly like, which continues making money even after they start drawing income. The golden handshake, the armload of documents, and how we help you deal with Medicare. When people walk out the company door for the last time, the HR Department loads them up with a ton of documents. They need to get on board with Medicare (Parts A and B in the jargon) and select private insurance companies to cover what Medicare does not (Parts C and D). There is some urgency. If you put off signing up for Medicare, hoping you can avoid paying premiums for a while, think again. If you have turned sixty-five and are not covered by an employer's health policy, well, you'll be sorry.

We'll help fill out the forms. There is an open window in the fall when you can switch carriers. If you feel your carrier has raised premiums by an excessive amount, more than age related, we'll run a new comparison for you. The coverages for each company are the same; what you want is a reliable carrier that charges you the least.

This is a popular service and we find that many clients take us up on it.

It runs in the family, on our side of the table and the clients' side as well.

Ours is a family firm. But look across the table. We tend to work with families a lot. We represented four generations— great-grandparent, grandparents, parents and son— until recently when the great-grandparent passed away. Their coverage varies by their life stage, of course, but just about every vehicle was represented. Annuities, estate planning, brokerage, life insurance.

We think the reason is that people trust us. This is what we do. This is where they are, and here is what they want to accomplish. What they want to accomplish is the most important thing.

Our slogan is: "Creating legacies, one family at a time."

Farmers Can't Take the Time to See Us, So We Go for Ride-Alongs

We offer a complimentary concierge service. What that means is we'll come out to their office, their home. We have a beautiful, spacious office in town. But they are more comfortable in their own setting. Nine times out of ten, they will take us up on it.

We're in Ohio farm country and farmers don't have the time to stop working. That makes for some interesting visits. Farmers with modern tractors, they have air conditioning, stereo, GPS—the tractor basically drives itself.

We jump in, chat, pass documents back and forth. Farmers with ancient tractors, well, not so much.

The three-bucket system, not to catch rain, but income for you. We sometimes use a three-bucket system to finance retirement which we believe is unique to us. Sort of a play on the old-fashioned grocery money in one envelope, rent money in another. The first bucket is for five years, the second for the next five years. When the first is empty, we turn to the second. The third bucket simply repeats the cycle. By the time we reach the third bucket, it has had ten years to grow.

The buckets are split one-quarter, one-quarter, one-half. The first uses an annuity with a 3 percent yield. The second bucket uses a different kind of annuity with a 4 percent yield. The third bucket uses equities with a growth target of 6 percent a year.

The concept is that the third bucket replenishes the other two when they are used up.

"I can live off 80 percent or 90 percent of my preretirement income, right?" Based on our experience, that might work for the first couple of years. Those first two years are really stressful and they are trying to penny pinch everything. Then they realize that retirement can be fun if they spend. Plus, life tends to throw in surprises. It's like a budget that looks fine on paper but try living with it.

Boomers, you need to put yourselves first. We'll show you how to solve the legacy worry, but repeat after us: "Retirement is a time for fun. Retirement is . . ."

If someone is struggling in retirement, do we ever have to give them the lecture, you have to take care of your needs first and not become a burden on your children?

Yes, all the time. Baby boomers may be living like paupers even though they have plenty of assets, hundreds of thousands or millions of dollars because they want to leave it all to their kids. They pay bills for their kids, a new truck for the grandkids. Meantime they may be limiting themselves to really just one meal a day.

You have to tell them that they must realize their own self-worth and their own quality of life are just as important as anyone else's. Even those they love. We want to take care of and protect our family, but we don't have to be in lopsided equations here.

There's a way to do that financially, to enjoy spending your money while still leaving a guaranteed amount of money, the amount that you specify, to your kids. That beauty is called life insurance. So you just tell us what the number is and we'll run the examples and the illustration. The vehicle is guaranteed universal life.

But once we get your children's money set up, you must promise us that you are going to take care of yourself. You're going to go out and have some fun. Sure, you can pay to have the roof fixed, but then you're going to do the things you want to do.

The universal life policy is more costly than for a twenty- or forty-year-old but we're still leveraging the money. If you put $100,000 in, we want to see it pay out a minimum of $200,000 and $300,000 makes us happier.

So basically, the legacy is in place for the kids. The parents are much more apt to stand up for themselves.

"Yes, I'm going to go play."

It is wonderful to see that transformation, the relief, to hear the sigh, to see the shoulders go down.

"It's done. I did it. Okay."

Downsizing, a way to stay young at heart, young in spirit, young in body. People may downsize immediately at retirement, perhaps buying a smaller house in a different state. They may move into an active seniors' complex after the passing of a spouse. Shifting to assisted care is like renting an apartment. Only with them doing the cooking and you get three square meals a day.

With activity centers, places to hang out. Everything on site from banking, massages, haircutting. Gyms with personal trainers. Excursions to entertainment.

In time skilled nursing or lockdowns (for Alzheimer's or dementia) can be arranged with adjustments in rent.

It is not cheap, Carol points out. One in Dublin, Ohio asks $500,000 up front for a couple with $50,000 a year in rent for five years. Life insurance policies eliminate financial risk from premature passing. It is definitely a premium service. They are getting what they pay for. I have visited clients three or six months after moving in. They have shifted from sitting on the couch to doing better, to enjoying life again. Their demeanor changes. They are standing a little taller. Their skin is a little brighter. Their outlook on life has changed dramatically.

There are two main things we must do right. First, we must spend the time to understand

Once they have made the decision, we help with adjusting their financial plan. I have been doing this a long time. Not once have we been unable to find a match with a facility they can afford.

Our introductory, fact-finding process is quite similar to the norm in the industry but crucial to finding the best end result. The most important aspect is looking at what the client is trying to accomplish. Then we shop that information around. Like for an insurance policy, you take all their information and you shop it among all the companies. So who wants to give the most coverage and charge them the least and kind of summarize that. It is a three-step process: Where are you now, where do you want to be and how can we get there? One, two, three.

There are two main things we must do right. First, we must spend the time to understand the client's needs and wants and their risk tolerance. Second, we must select the right products and sufficient strategies to match them. For every plan we come up with, we check on their medical coverage. We want to make sure the entire plan does not collapse because of some medical issue.

We put on seminars, rotating among three retirement topics. But no seminar ever runs more than an hour. We see the clients' eyes glaze over. We think we hear the bell ringing now.

One last thought: We measure our success in the level of our client's happiness. And we're very good at it. This is why they pass us along to other family members, to friends. We do the referral business that we do because we do what we say and we say what we'll do.

About the Authors

Bryan Foster
CEO
BFFinancial

Carol Carroll
Senior Vice President
BFFinancial

Bryan Foster is chief executive officer of BFFinancial in Dublin, Ohio. Carol Carroll is senior vice president. More commonly, they are known as son and mother. BFFinancial Advisors of Dublin, Ohio, should not be confused with a firm of the same name in another state. Look for them at bffinancialadvisors.com or pick up the phone and call 614-789-1644.

It's Your Life and Your Money: Plan Ahead for Your Retirement

by Ben Fuchs

After spending much of your adult life working hard and saving as much as possible, you may be thinking about retirement. People who plan to retire in the next ten years should take steps now to be as prepared as possible for the day when they finally decide to step away from their careers and enjoy the fruits of their labor.

First, ask yourself a few key questions that will help you chart the path for your phase of life:

1. What kind of lifestyle do you want to lead in retirement?

2. Should you eliminate all debt before you retire?

3. Are there investments you should consider now that will minimize taxes when you retire?

4. What can you do now to minimize the impact of economic downturns?

5. Do you want to spend it all or leave something for the next generation or charities?

Considering these and other related questions now will allow you to work with an investment advisor over time to position your portfolio so that the retirement you actually experience is in line with the retirement you desire.

Target the Life You Want

You may assume that once you retire, your need for income will diminish. In many cases, this assumption is inaccurate. While some people will experience lower costs per year as they no longer pay for their kids' college tuition, support loved ones, or pay down debt, people often find their spending habits keep up with their changes in lifestyle. Ultimately, you may find that your retirement is as costly, or more costly, on a yearly basis as your pre-retirement life was.

Whatever your plans may be for retirement—travel or buying a second home—your investment advisor should work with you to find investment options that will support the life you want to lead. They should also help you plan for unanticipated expenses, like healthcare costs from major surgeries or long-term care expenses for yourself, your parents, or other loved ones.

Be honest and realistic with yourself when you meet with your advisor. Consider all the things you want to do with the next phase of your life, as well as any speedbumps that may come up along the way that could potentially derail your plans. Expect to spend at least as much over the first five years of retirement as you spend each year prior to retiring. Adjust this strategy over time as your specific needs require.

Give yourself a cushion, as well, that is large enough to absorb any blows your portfolio will take over the course of time. Your good health, and that of your family members, is something to consider as you plan. Healthcare costs are an inevitability in life and will become more likely as you age. Caring for parents or loved ones who cannot care for themselves is often a concern. Your advisor can help you prepare for these kinds of expenses by maintaining a portfolio flexible enough to generate cash when needed and provide growth of your investments when it is not.

Managing Debt Is Not the Same Thing as Eliminating It

As you were growing up and beginning your adult life, you likely received well-meaning advice from trusted people in your life, such as parents, work colleagues, or friends. These people may have suggested that eliminating all debt prior to retirement was a tried and true formula for future success. Often this strategy makes quite a bit of sense, but not always.

In the late 70s and early 80s, when our parents were in the latter half of their careers and turning their own eyes toward retirement, interest rates were very high and the cost of debt made it particularly important to avoid carrying debt of any kind into retirement.

Today, however, interest rates are at historic lows. The cost of debt is often affordable to pre-retirees and even retirees when compared to the average rate of return their portfolio can generate. Talk with your advisor about debt and its overall impact on your portfolio. You may find you are better off letting your portfolio pay down your debt over time while keeping your assets where they belong: invested in your future.

Life Knows but Two Inevitabilities

It may be true that you can't avoid your own mortality; it catches up with everyone eventually. But the need to pay taxes is not truly an inevitability. National and state tax rules and regulations allow for a fair amount of flexibility when considering your portfolio of investments as well as their eventual liquidation.

Discuss with your advisor, in advance of your retirement, how your assets will be taxed in the future. Depending on your age, your finances, and the state in which you reside, the impact of your tax burden could be significant.

These are a few ways to minimize taxable income as you approach and begin your retirement journey.

1. Maximize Retirement Savings

If your company offers an employer-sponsored retirement savings plan, such as a 401(k) or 403(b), you can make pre-tax contributions up to a maximum of $19,500 in 2020. If you are 50+ years old, you can make additional *catch-up* contributions of up to $6,500 each year as well.

These kinds of contributions are made on a pretax basis, so the money saved in your employer-sponsored retirement account lowers your tax bill each year you contribute.

If you don't have the option to save through an employer-sponsored plan, all is not lost. Your contributions to a traditional individual retirement account (IRA) can be a great alternative. The maximum contribution to an IRA in 2020 is $6,000 per year, with a catch-up provision of up to $1,000 each year for people who are age 50 or older.

If you or your spouse work for companies with employer-sponsored retirement plans, you may also be able to deduct some or all of your traditional IRA contributions from your state and federal taxes. Speak with your investment advisor or a qualified tax advisor about this possibility.

2. Contribute to Flexible Spending Plans

Many employers offer flexible spending plans (FSAs) or health savings accounts (HSAs) that allow you to minimize taxable income by setting aside a portion of your earnings in a separate account managed by an employer.

With most insurance plans, you can contribute $2750 in 2020 to an FSA, if offered by your employer. With an HSA, available only to employees with high deductible health insurance plans, you can contribute up to $3,550 per year for an individual, or families can contribute up to $7100 per year.

Both FSAs and HSAs provide for a reduction in tax bills during the years in which contributions are made.

3. Keep More Capital From Your Gains

You can also plan for events that require the sale of assets in order to minimize the taxes you will have to pay on your capital gains.

A capital gains tax is assessed on the positive difference between the sale price of an asset and its original purchase price.

Short-term capital gains taxes apply to profits from the sale of assets held for a year or less. These profits are taxed as ordinary income. Long-term capital gains taxes are based on the profits from the sale of assets held for more than a year. The long-term capital gains tax can be as high as 20 percent, depending on your tax bracket.

Timing the sale of assets allows you to minimize the capital gains by offsetting these gains with a capital loss—the sale of an asset at a lower price than its original purchase price. By choosing to sell an underperforming asset in conjunction with assets that will realize a capital gain, you offset the gain and minimize your tax burden.

Work with your advisor to formulate a long-term strategy to manage the sale of assets for any reason. Planning ahead allows you to minimize paying unnecessary and costly income taxes and ultimately keep more of your hard-earned money.

Spread the Wealth, Literally

When the economy is firing on all cylinders, it feels like you can't go wrong with your portfolio strategy; as the market goes up, so go your profits. But what if the market hits a trough? What if there is a global event like a pandemic or natural catastrophe that impacts the U.S. or global economies?

You can never be sure of what the market will do at any moment, so you can't forget the importance of a balanced, or diversified, portfolio that minimizes your exposure to risk when the market struggling. And don't try to time the market. Gambling with your investments is not a strategy. Instead, plan for the natural ebb and flow that economies often experience.

Your investment advisor should have discussed diversification with you. If not, ask about it. Savvy investors should never put all their eggs—or in this case, investments—in one basket. Avoid a portfolio that is entirely invested in, or too heavily weighted toward, one asset class, such as securities or stocks.

Look instead for asset classes that have low or negative correlations: if one moves up, the other tends to do the opposite.

Mutual funds are a common and easy way to select asset classes that will diversify your portfolio. Be aware of hidden costs and trading commissions with these kinds of investments. Also remember to diversify your investments from a single family of funds, such as America Funds or Fidelity. These are fine options, but focusing too much of your portfolio in one fund family also puts your portfolio's health at unnecessary risk.

Many people choose to evolve their mix of asset classes over time. Advisors will often ask if you want to take an aggressive or a conservative approach. When these questions are asked of you, their goal is to understand what percentage of your assets should be held in more conservative investments, like bonds or bank products, versus more aggressive investments, like stocks that are subject to more rapid swings in value based on factors like company performance or swings in the overall economy.

The key to setting the right parameters for your overall investment strategy is to evolve your portfolio as your needs and desires evolve. Your investment advisor can guide you toward the many ways to balance and diversify your portfolio to ensure the mix of investments is right for you, both today and in the future.

You Can't Take It With You

One final consideration that should be discussed with your advisor is whether your portfolio should be designed to carry on beyond your death. This is important to understand because investment strategies are different if you desire to leave wealth to your children or another entity rather than spending it in your lifetime.

You may sometimes see or hear your investment strategy incorrectly referred to as *estate planning*. True estate planning involves certain legal constructs beyond your investments and other assets. An estate plan can include a generational wealth strategy geared toward the disposition of your assets after you die. Creating a generational wealth strategy involves long-term planning of investments designed to maximize a return on those investments for the benefit of others rather than for yourself.

There is no right answer to the question of whether to spend it all or leave some to others. The choice to plan for generational wealth, or not, is a very personal decision. Be honest with yourself and your advisor regarding your goals. And make sure you keep your advisor in the loop should your thoughts on this issue change. It's your money, so do with it what you so desire.

Most people find a comfortable balance between supporting their near-term, individual needs for supplemental income with a longer-term goal to leave a portion of their wealth to others. Your advisor can work with you to target a percentage of your portfolio to invest differently in order to maximize the amount you will ultimately leave to your children, to charities, or both.

In Conclusion

If you remember nothing else from reading this chapter, please remember this:

1. Take ownership of your retirement strategy and chart a path based on your short- and long-term needs and desires.

2. Listen to others who can offer their guidance and expertise but hold true to your specific goals and evolve them over time as your perspective changes.

3. While focused on the lifestyle you want to lead in retirement, remain actively involved in and make informed decisions about how your money is invested.

Most importantly, enjoy this next phase of your life!

About the Author

Ben Fuchs
Founder
Fuchs Financial

Ben Fuchs, a Certified Financial Planner (CFP) with more than fifteen years of investment experience, has created thousands of retirement plans. His focus is on maintaining income in retirement and structuring portfolios to withstand inevitable market crashes. Mr. Fuchs strives to understand each client's individual retirement goals and creates plans to achieve them. He believes that clients should understand where their retirement income comes from and ensure they have the peace of mind that a tailored financial strategy brings.

Fuchs Financial, LLC is focused on providing short- and long-term planning services, so money is one less thing for you to worry about in your retirement.

Making Retirement Financially Successful

by Victor J. Gray

One of the most important factors of our lives is our finances. You could put ahead of that your spiritual life, health, physical life, and relationships, but they are all impacted by your financial life. Making your financial life successful can also aid other areas of your life.

Your finances should not be a cause of stress to you. Your finances should be adequate to accomplish what you want in life. As well, your finances can make it possible to achieve your goals in relation with other people. It can facilitate you visiting children and grandchildren far away, for example. You do not want to be in a position of not being able to visit or be in relationship the way you want to be. So, your financial situation could aid your total fulfillment of every aspect of your successful retirement.

In creating a financially successful retirement, there is no right or wrong. *Success* is determined by whether you have gained what you want for yourself and your family. You get to make the decisions. You determine what is successful for you. To achieve this, you need to know what you want to do, and craft a plan on how to get there, including an income plan, an asset plan, and a legacy plan. They together form your financial success.

You can do it. You just have to create realistic and proper plans. A financial advisor can help you with this process.

What is realistic and proper?

How do you keep your financial plans from being derailed by elements you cannot control?

Since we cannot know exactly what the future holds, no financial plan is 100 percent guaranteed, but you can make your plan work for you and your family. It has been said that the proper plan leads to the proper results. You get to determine what results are *desired* for you. I want to help you attain the results you desire. Creating your financial plan is like writing a book: you get to write the end chapter; you get to write the finish the way that you want it to be.

How to Not Stress Over Your Financial Future

The first step in not stressing over your financial future is, of course, to have adequate income. They say that income in retirement is similar to oxygen. You have to have it. You may be wondering what will happen to your assets in a volatile market that is going up and down. You may worry that you won't have enough money to last the rest of your life. Those concerns, of course, can make retirement extremely stressful. You want to eliminate that stress—it can damage your health. You want to make sure that as you get older, you have adequate and good healthcare, you are cared for, and you can live out your life in a manner that is suitable. Income during retirement makes that possible.

You also need to know what an acceptable amount of risk is to take, not only financially but emotionally. Make sure you are well informed, so you are not caught by surprise. Work with your advisor to assess the risk you can accept regarding your holdings, your investments, and your income.

Do you have adequate money to live the lifestyle that you want?

Can you do it in the manner you want to?

These are important questions to ask because not being able to do things—or worrying about not being able to do things—can be devastating to your financial picture and to your physical health.

Be willing to say no to things that are outside your goals, or be willing to decline anything that does not fit your financial profile. Do not get caught in a dilemma in which you are being engaged by something too costly or find yourself in uncomfortable situations you cannot live with. You can be in total control of your assets between you and your spouse, children, or whomever. Making appropriate decisions will help lower the likelihood of being stressed by your finances.

Know Your Individual Risk Profile

Knowing your risk level is really about being in control. In determining your individual risk profile, I ask a series of questions about hypothetical situations. There are so many circumstances we just cannot control.

Risks—financial and otherwise—can include:

- Long-term care and end-of-life care
- Accident or injury
- Enough income to pay your cost of living
- Unforeseen expenses to support a family member
- Sudden downward fluctuations in stock market
- Mistakes in financial judgment or management

We want to make sure that, no matter what happens, you understand your situation, and you have decided ahead of time how you can respond should any of the risks become a reality.

We never know exactly what is going to happen in the future. Part of preparing for the unknown is assessing what level of risk is tolerable to you. A major point I'd like to make here is that as you create your retirement plan, it is okay to have *no* risk. Risk level is up to each individual person or couple. Your financial advisor can help you figure out what that means and how it will affect your retirement.

- What level of risk are you at now, and how much risk you are willing to accept, if any?

- If you want your money at no risk, how is it going to work?

- Will you be able to do the things you want and not worry about having monies or income at risk?

Once you have found the right level of risk for you, be at that amount of risk. Be at the right amount of risk for yourself, and make sure that your investments match that level of risk. If you are married, you and your spouse should understand your finances together and be on the same track. If you have obligations to help family—parents, children, whomever—make sure that you have adequate resources set aside. You want to meet your goals and to ensure you are not stressing over things that you cannot do or cannot afford.

Do not take on something that is going to put you in a position of where you feel like you made a mistake. Because mistakes in retirement generally are difficult to undo.

Because you cannot know what is going to happen, know that you can take care of whatever comes your way. Work with your advisor to make it possible to be in control by making sure your finances are taken care of, you know exactly where you want to be, and you know how you are going to get there.

One thing many retirees have in common is they generally never want to go back to work. If they do return to work, it is because they *want* to, not because they *have* to.

Things You Cannot Control

In a perfect world, we would be able to predict how life unfolds. We could predict rates of return, prepare for all kinds of hypothetical situations, and feel confident everything would turn out wonderfully.

But the reality is, there are things we cannot control:

- Interest rates rising and falling
- Higher taxes
- Shift of political administrations
- Changes in health
- Worldwide pandemic

We want to know we can be safe from the things we cannot control. They may get us involved when we did not plan on being involved. They may get us involved when we did not want to get involved but needed to. We want to know we'll still be okay financially.

Plan your response to events you cannot control. Strategize how you will take care of those situations. The only way to stay safe from the things that we cannot control is to install contingency plans.

Is Your Income Adequate to Last Your Lifetime?

One of the ways you can prepare for retirement is to ensure adequate income to be able to live the way you want, to have the things you need, and to receive the healthcare you require. So many outside components can change your income, such as interest rates. I know when I first got into this business, the average interest rate on a CD was anywhere from 8 to 10 percent, and today is 1 to 2 percent. Well, my goodness! If you had a retirement that was predicated on needing to get an 8 to 10 percent guaranteed, with a no-risk rate of return, and now you are getting a fraction of that, well, that would be devastating.

You need to devise an income plan that works regardless of the outside influences. We can plan for certain events, so if they do ultimately come to pass, you will still have income to last the rest of your life.

We offer a complimentary consultation for potential clients, and when I do reviews, I see many people have a beautiful plan. It works just fine. They are living the way they want to live; their income is secure. The problem is that it will last for only a certain period of time.

Maybe they are seventy years old, and their income plan is perfect for ten years. But if they have a life expectancy of eighty-six years plus, their income is going to stop at eighty. What do they do from eighty to eighty-six, or for the rest of their life, if they live to be ninety-six?

Your plan has to be such that it lasts as long as you do. In a nutshell, you cannot count on dying. You cannot have an income plan that only works for a certain period of time. It has to work indefinitely. You might be one of those people who has tremendous longevity, living to ninety, ninety-five, maybe even one hundred years old.

Are you going to still be okay?

Are you going to be able to pay bills, eat, take care of yourself, have somebody help take care of you?

It is easy to know when we are going to retire, but we have to stay retired, and stay retired, living the lifestyle that we want to live.

Is your retirement going to last as long as you do?

Guaranteed lifetime income is something people ought to consider. It's a way to make sure that you cannot outlive your income.

How Important to You Is Leaving an Inheritance?

On a scale of one to ten—one being the lowest, ten being the highest—how important is leaving an inheritance or legacy for family, loved ones, and causes that you are concerned about?

Rate how important it is. Leaving an inheritance is something that you have to plan. We may have loved ones who are dependent on us. Spouses need to consider leaving an inheritance because there is generally a loss of income when the first spouse dies, whether it is due to loss of social security, pension, or whatever funds were used in end-of-life healthcare.

As your financial advisor, I need to know what you want to provide for others to factor in your assets in a balanced way. If you say leaving an inheritance is at a ten, but your program spends all your money, you will not reach your financial goals. And, it is so important that you meet your financial goals.

If inheritance—leaving a legacy to your family when you pass on—is important, you need to do it in advance. The way to accomplish that is to make your legacy plan just as important as your income plan, your asset plan, and your healthcare plan.

We certainly are in unprecedented times. I do not know what the future will bring. In these uncertain times, families may need a little help. When we are no longer here to provide that helping hand, leaving an inheritance could fulfill a great need. In the past, it may have been the extras—the leftover funds—that were extended in legacy planning, but now, an inheritance may be the only retirement plan that the next generation has. With rising taxes, expenses going up, inflation, your gift may be very much needed for certain family members. They may need that legacy that you can set aside for them.

About the Author

Victor Gray
Founder
Victor Gray Financial Services

Victor Gray is now in his fourth decade in the financial services industry, having provided valuable financial services, plans, and information to countless families and individuals. His genuine concern for clients' well-being and vast knowledge of the industry motivates him to help clients meet their challenges, needs, and desires. His emphasis is not only on quality of information and plans provided to those he serves, but also on the service and relationships provided.

Dedicating his life's work to clients' financial service needs, his goal is to continually improve his clients' financial position through individualized plans tailored to specific needs and concerns.

With over thirty years' experience, education, and a dedication to needs, he is helping many people obtain their desired results.

Victor and his wife, Clara Ines, live in Warren County, Ohio, with their two daughters.

Investment Strategies and Principles to Help You Navigate and Simplify Investing for Retirement

by Michael Russo

Many people do not know where to begin when they want to invest for retirement. You may have questions, such as:

- *What is an appropriate plan?*
- *What investment vehicles should I use?*
- *Whose financial advice should I listen to?*

Since your needs and investment objectives may be different from someone else's, the plan you put together should be tailored to your particular situation. Investing for retirement doesn't have to be difficult. This content is to help you navigate the complex world of investing and simplify it, to help you have a successful retirement.

Asset Class Investing

A key to successful long-term investing is having proper asset allocation and diversification in your investment portfolio. Typically, the first thing an investor does is figure out what percentage of your investment goes into stocks, bonds, cash, or other asset classes.

There are two questions that the investor needs to answer:

1. What is your time horizon for the investment?

2. What is your risk tolerance?

Once those questions are answered, they put together a portfolio. It can include many different asset classes, investing in:

- Small, medium, and large companies
- Developed international companies
- Emerging market companies
- Growth companies
- Value companies
- Real estate

Owning different asset classes helps diversity your investment portfolio. When your portfolio is diversified among different asset classes, it helps protect your portfolio when the markets correct, while also potentially capturing the returns in rising markets.

To share a story, someone came into our office in January of 2019. Their investment portfolio was overweighted and had over 50 percent of their equity holdings in developed international and emerging market securities. Now, it just so happened that those were two of the worst-performing asset classes in 2018.[1] If this investor had diversified and weighted their portfolio—among different asset classes—based on their risk profile, their investment losses would have been significantly less than what they experienced.

I believe the key to asset class investing is to limit your losses when the markets correct or fall. By limiting your losses when the markets are down, you really do not need to chase high rates of return. This can help reduce risk in your portfolio.

The Importance of Rebalancing Your Investment Portfolio

Many investors take for granted the importance of rebalancing their portfolios. But, rebalancing your portfolio is probably one of the most critical things you can do. It allows you to maintain a desired asset allocation over a period of time. You're strategically buying and selling assets in a portfolio, not only to keep a desired asset allocation, but also to help mitigate risk in the portfolio.

An investor came into our office this past December. He had set up a portfolio five years before, following recommendations based on his risk profile. It determined he should have 65 percent of his money in stocks and equities, and the other 35 percent of his holding should be in bonds and fixed

1 "The Callan Periodic table of Investment Returns: 2000—2019. *Callan.* callan.com/wp-content/uploads/2020/01/Classic-Periodic-Table.pdf

income. Originally, he rolled over a 401(k). He invested it, but then took no other action for five years. When we did an analysis of his portfolio, he now had close to 88 percent of his holdings in equities and stocks, and only 12 percent were in bonds and fixed income. By not rebalancing and letting his portfolio grow as it did, he increased the risk of his portfolio.

Rebalancing is not only about making sure your overall asset allocation is in line, but also about making sure the portfolio does not become too dependent upon one particular asset class, stock, or bond. We generally recommend you rebalance at set intervals of time or when a particular asset class is out of equilibrium. We believe it should be done at least semiannually, annually, or if any asset class changes by 5 percent in either direction. Rebalancing can help maintain the integrity of the portfolio.

Active Versus Passive Money Management
There seems to be an ongoing debate in our industry about which is a better style of investing or management.

Are *active money management or passive money management* strategies better?

Active management strategies require the portfolio manager to buy and sell securities to outperform the market or a specific market index. If you practice active money management, you watch different market trends or shifts in the economy, and try to time buying and selling specific securities accordingly.

Since you are trying to beat the market, it could be argued that actively managed accounts tend to have greater risks than passively managed accounts.

Passive money management can also be referred to as *index investing*. The goal of this management is to generate a rate of return that mirrors a market return or a specific market index benchmark. With passive money management, the fees may be lower than those for active money management. Certain actively managed accounts generate a lot more trading activity, and that can result in higher charges that are passed through to the investor. Historically, when the market has been volatile, active money management strategies may outperform passive money management strategies more often than not. When specific securities or asset classes are moving within unison or are highly correlated, passive money management strategies may be the better way to go.

As you get closer to retirement or as you enter retirement, a combination of both strategies could be used. This way, even in a bull market, both strategies will perform. But, if you are retired and you are experiencing a volatile market or you are in a market correction when you retire, actively managed portfolios can help leverage your risk, and certain actively managed portfolios have the ability to go to cash. They can help limit your investment losses, losses you may not be able to afford in retirement.

Investing in Exchange Traded Funds and Mutual Funds

Investors generally try to invest in a vast array of available funds. Those funds can include:

- Exchange traded funds
- Index mutual funds
- Actively managed mutual funds

Exchange traded funds trade like stocks and are generally more passive investments. Since they operate in a passive style, they may result in lower internal fees and expenses that the investor pays. They also tend to be more tax efficient than other available funds.

Most *mutual funds* are not bought on an exchange, they are purchased directly from an investment company. In general, mutual funds have higher internal expenses than exchange traded funds. Many investors now come into our office and buy index mutual funds that track a particular market index. Investors will buy these because they can have lower fees and expenses, and there is virtually very little monitoring that is needed, since they track the market. But the investors have no control of what the index is investing in. Since you are holding the actual market index, you are a participant in the entire correction when there is a major market correction that affects the index.

In actively managed mutual funds, the active money managers try to outperform their benchmarks, so the managers generally do more buying than selling of the securities in the fund as they analyze different economic and market trends. Actively managed mutual funds generally come with higher fees, and they are also less tax efficient than index funds and exchange traded funds.

Many new clients come into our office holding exchange traded funds, index mutual funds, and actively managed mutual funds, but have no strategy on how they put together their portfolio. This is where the advice of a financial advisor comes into play—where a financial advisor can help properly construct a diversified portfolio that meets the client's needs and objectives for the opportunity of long-term investment success.

Challenges of Investing in Fixed Income Securities in Retirement

Fixed income is actually an asset class that many investors have in their portfolio, and the reason we believe they have it is for stability. In my experience, many investors hold fixed income in their portfolio for diversification, to preserve capital, to generate income, and for inflation protection. But as you approach retirement—and even in retirement—you may depend on the income generated from the fixed income and bonds investments.

Your diversified portfolio may include:

- Government bonds

- Corporate bonds
- Municipal bonds
- Bond funds
- REITs
- Annuities

Investing in fixed income securities and bonds is not as easy as it used to be. A current problem is that interest rates are low, and these traditional fixed income investments are not generating enough income to provide for retirees. Investors now have to rethink how they view traditional fixed income. They need to implement strategies that can potentially achieve a better rate of return on fixed income in their pre-retiree years *and* generate the desired income they need in their retirement years.

We believe it is important to construct a retirement plan for clients and to take into account the changing economic conditions, market conditions, and inflation. Lacking these considerations, we risk developing a plan that strands clients without enough income in retirement.

We believe an excellent retirement income distribution plan must:

- Ensure that a client has a certain amount of guaranteed income

- Be flexible

- Allow for income to be generated from varying assets based on different economic and market conditions in retirement

As you enter retirement, we feel your portfolio needs to be constructed to include a growth element in retirement and a fixed income element. When investing in fixed income in your pre-retirement years, consider working with a financial advisor to help you put together a diversified portfolio.

About the Author

Michael Russo
Chief Financial Officer
Millstone Financial Group

Mike has more than twenty-eight years of experience in the financial services industry, including more than ten years as an Investment Advisor Representative. This experience has afforded Mike the knowledge to help his clients meet their financial and retirement goals. At Millstone Financial Group, Mike's purpose is to educate his clients about the investments they own and present every client with what he believes are sound investment management philosophies and retirement distribution strategies.

Mike graduated from Montclair State University with a degree in business administration, majoring in finance. He immediately went to work on Wall Street for Brown

Brothers Harriman. During his tenure at Brown Brothers Harriman, Mike was recruited to work as an asset-based financial advisor at Metlife, where he spent the next twelve years. It was there he developed his passion for the financial markets, portfolio analysis, and asset allocation.

Mike's main responsibility is managing the firm's assets. He is an Investment Advisor Representative and a Fiduciary, which means he's legally obligated to do what is in the best interest of the client, always. Above all else, Mike's goals are to help clients reduce overall risk exposures and create personalized investment management strategies.

Mike was raised in a modest household where family always came first. He attributes his success to both of his parents, who were hardworking. They instilled core values and integrity, which he prides himself on every day.

Mike has been married to his wife, Maryann, since 1992. They reside in Howell with their three children, Matt, Craig, and Kellie. Mike is an avid sports fan and golfer. He is also a member of Battleground Country Club and enjoys being out on the course or having dinner with good friends and clients.

"It Was The Right Thing To Do"

by Paul Taylor

Once in my thirty-year career I worked for a large brokerage firm. You know the kind. They have offices across the nation. They advertise constantly. They have become household names. Me, I had all the necessary licenses, both on the insurance side and the equities side.

A principal in the firm asked me to do something that was not right for the client. I resigned as quickly as I could get my office affairs in order. It was the right thing to do. I have never looked back.

I became an independent man with my own independent firm. I became a fiduciary.

I'm Paul Taylor. Today I run Capital Advisory Group, a boutique financial services firm in a beautiful part of North Carolina. Mooresville is our home base. It's on Lake Norman, stretching across several counties.

Many of our clients have recently relocated here. And why not? It is an easy commute to the headquarters of major firms. Cultural activities are abundant. There is room to move around in for those who enjoy the outdoors. Count me among those who can be found boating, golfing, or bird hunting in leisure hours.

Capital Advisory Group, with five employees, is small. Don't let that fool you. We have eight or nine investment professionals we call on for their particular expertise and also get support from a second-generation Michigan investment firm. We have an affiliation, too, with Morningstar, Inc. so their extensive database is available to us.

I get asked—often—about what is special about our firm. I'm proud to answer. Our mission statement: "The Lord God is the center of our business. Through this belief we strive to make a difference in our clients' lives by doing more than financial planning." It's the foundation of my values and my passion for those I am blessed to serve.

Get to know me a little more by visiting our website, www. capitaladvisorygroup.net. It contains brief videos of me explaining who we are and how we can help. As stated, family is very important to me. The website will also share with you those closest to me—my wife and children. In one video I share a passion that my wife Rena and I share hosting clients for a boat ride or a meal at our house with me doing the cooking (It's a creative release for me).

At Capital Advisory Group we measure success not in bottom-line profits but in how we help people transition into retirement.

We are fiduciaries, who put the client's interest first, just as I did in my choice of employers. Only about 49 percent of people in our industry work as fiduciaries, according to a 2017 FINRA study. We don't answer to anybody except you. We have access to everything, not just a few products with some of them possibly overpriced. We're very boutique, because every client's needs are different. We take everyone's situation and look at it individually. We don't have a standard cure. Everyone needs to have a true financial plan that's going to meet their goals and objectives.

As a fiduciary, we work on a fee-based basis. Insurance products are sometimes the right answer for a client. Any time you work with an insurance company, built-in commissions are hard to avoid. However, we always seek to work in our clients' best interests, finding products that are the right fit for them. We're not persuaded to sell some insurance product based on the commissions the carriers pay us; putting your needs first is our priority.

At Capital Advisory Group, my staff of five is my back office. I'm the quarterback who pulled the team together.

The goal is to create a game plan. Someone comes in with all their records for an introductory session on the first appointment. We listen as they tell us their goals and what their challenge may be. We look at their investment history and run an analysis of the risk involved in their current holdings. We run a full background check on every single item in the portfolio. We will see what their income needs are and analyze, number one, the chances they might run out of money. Number two, based on their answers, we'll say whether they have more or less risk than we believe is prudent.

The following is a general description of services offered to illustrate how we serve clients, and not a discussion of specific product or security recommendations.

We vary our solutions to the client's circumstances and goals. There are some common concepts we apply. Consider, for example, a hypothetical couple of average means who are conservative and do not want to outlive their money.

We might suggest a three-bucket system. The first bucket would be for immediate income. This would be a one- to five-year bucket of short-term bonds or comparables for income over the next five years. We would then set up two other buckets. One would have more opportunity for growth. It would replenish anything we had placed in bucket one for income. Bucket three would be for extreme growth. It is designed not to be touched for at least ten years.

We consider where we are in the economic cycle before we craft a retirement plan for you. We want to make sure you have the proper mix in your portfolio. In today's low-interest environment, we might shy away from long-duration bonds. There may be another rate cut or two, but interest rates have to rise. The government is $22 trillion in debt and owners of government obligations will demand more interest on their money.

Everyone is different but many have similar concerns. Let's look at some of the questions or situations they present.

I'm often asked what we do if another 2008 comes along.

A cardinal rule is that we design a well-diversified account to begin with. I don't like for 100 percent of the assets to be in the stock market, ever. We will make changes in the portfolio when there is clear direction and there were clear directions in '08. So we are not averse to going to cash (money markets) and being patient. If a client is late in accepting that realization, we tell them they might as well stay in because the damage has been done and pulling out now would be the dumbest thing they could do. Prospective clients want to know if we have an account minimum and the answer is easy: $250,000.

Financially sophisticated people, in particular, ask what products we use for the risky side of the portfolio. We might consider exchange traded funds (ETFs). They don't have the old-fashioned restrictive rules that mutual funds carry, number one. Number two, we might consider trading those ETFs virtually free through any of the major brokerages.

Some new clients arrive with portfolios that, frankly, are a mess. Perhaps they have bounced around the country from place to place as their career called for. They may have had several advisors over the years.

We do a portfolio analysis to show, hey this is where you are, here are the risks you have taken, your standard deviation (a measure of volatility) and the rate of return you have received.

Before we propose a solution, however, we identify any assets they are married to that have highly appreciated.

Many about-to-be retirees are concerned about what the economy may do in the first year or two of their retirement. What happens if it takes a nosedive?

It is true that if the market rises when you retire you're going to be fine and if the market turns down you may struggle for a long time.

An important part of that, however, is being realistic in what you withdraw each year.

You should never have 100 percent of your portfolio exposed to risk. You should have your portfolio protected in such a way that if the market is down, you can pull from the protected side.

There are clients who must make their funds last an exceptionally long time. Such as a husband with a considerably younger wife or a couple with a grown child with special needs.

A life insurance policy might be a great way to plan for that—if you can afford it. Your retirement plan needs to be built in a way that addresses, "Am I going to have enough money for the long retirement?" If not, we need to have this conversation anyway. You have to reduce your spending, go to plan B. How do you want to tackle that? A life insurance policy may still be the answer. If you don't have enough money to pay the premium, you work on reducing your spending to get enough assets to pay the premium.

Some clients can be too frugal in retirement, reluctant to dip into ample savings to splurge just a little on themselves.

Financial freedom during retirement is oh so nice. But so is financial freedom all through life. When I can reach millennials directly or through their parents or grandparents, I preach: "Live below your means."

About the Author

Paul Taylor
Founder
Capital Advisory Group

Paul Taylor founded Capital Advisory Group twenty years ago. He is a fiduciary and was accepted as a member of the National Ethics Bureau in 2007. He is married with three children. There is another company with a similar name so look for him at capitaladvisorygroup.net. Or, phone him at 704-947-6985.

His online video snippets give a feel for what his firm is like and strive to put you at ease the moment you walk in the door. Investment advisory and financial planning services offered through Advisory Alpha, LLC, a SEC Registered Investment Advisor. Insurance, consulting, and education services are offered through Capital Advisory Group. Advisory Alpha

Conclusion

Simply put, American retirees and pre-retirees do not have enough access to great information from valid sources. Not all financial advisors are created equal, and we have specifically selected the advisors in this book based on their expertise in their industries. Wherever you are in your journey as a retiree or pre-retiree, you can bring their sound advice to your current advisor or apply it on your own. This book is a collection of knowledge that you can apply to make prudent decisions for you and your family to retire on your terms.

From the twelve advisors featured in this book, you get twelve golden nuggets that will translate directly into a piece of your retirement. We want you to be able to connect the dots so that you and your family have the opportunity to retire well. So many families today will either live a mediocre retirement or a very difficult retirement. Please apply the collective wisdom in this book to create the retirement of your dreams.

Most American retirees and pre-retirees just do not know where to start. They have trusted their advisor consistently through good times and bad times. They are not really sure how to make good course corrections or ask the appropriate questions of their current advisory team to make sure their retirement will attain their respective goals and dreams. My hope is that while reading this book you have made notes, highlighted, or flagged the ideas that pertain to you and your family. I hope you have discovered action points here that will help you change the trajectory of your retirement for the better.

Clearly it is in your best interest to follow up with the person who gave you this book because they have demonstrated their desire to educate the public by taking time, energy, money, and resources to share the information you need to retire well.

In summary, my hopes are that each of you reading this book will take some sort of action. Unfortunately, so few people take action once they have been given the appropriate information to better themselves. I challenge you today to take in the information you have received in this book and use it to better your circumstances, as well as your family and your legacy. That is my hope for all of you.

About the Editor

Mark Gaffney

Mark is the Founder of MEG, a boutique marketing, coaching, and consulting firm for the financial services industry. Mark's Elite Advisor Client List reads like a *Who's Who* of financial advisory firms. Since 2002, he has coached, consulted, and trained thousands of financial professionals across the United States. His image and brand advertising agency approach to financial marketing has made him a prominent authority throughout the national advisor community.

With more than twenty-five years' experience in marketing, Mark's list of credits include: renowned national marketing strategist, executive producer of numerous television shows and radio programs across the United States, keynote speaker, and co-author of the best-seller, *The Winning Way*.

Mark has worked with multi-billion-dollar corporations as well as startups and financial business entrepreneurs at all phases of development. His marketing strategies have generated billions in production for his financial clients.